...of a sudden

Ray Liversidge

...of a sudden

To Tess, and love late in life

…of a sudden
ISBN 978 1 76109 490 3
Copyright © text Ray Liversidge 2023
Cover image: Terri Redpath

First published 2023 by
Ginninderra Press
PO Box 3461 Port Adelaide 5015 Australia
www.ginninderrapress.com.au

Contents

He hinted he might consider moving	9
Every river	10
One wonders	11
They come down	12
no water no bridge	13
It is yet to be determined	14
There may be some flaws in this story	15
Right now they missed lying	16
It was in the days before streets	17
Leaving the café	18
Sometimes I don't feel comfortable writing	19
Some six hours after meeting	20
It's not that he still didn't desire	21
disspooned	23
Friends asked her	24
When the quiz show host	26
He thought the opening line	27
It is hoped this story	28
Imagine if you can this story	29
If there were a need for a story	30
This turns out to be	31
Rothko	32
Tanka	33
The landscape	34
Far off the world	35
I really shouldn't	36
She had positioned herself	37
Maybe we should cut	38
Simileless	39
Fall	40

Speech therapy	41
She said,	42
At first I thought	43
Ask you (said quickly)	45
Post Pompeii, Hiroshima, Apocalypse	46
In the zone	47
There are several scars in this story	48
He loved live theatre and bled easily	50
'What side of the bed do you want?' he asked her.	51
Back then he was mesmerised by them –	52
The pimple was pissed off	53
White angels	54
To sleep, perchance	55
Requiem	56
We ask	57
She took a seat	58
Always	59
The sea (is dead)	60
From the moment	61
Being smaller than the other two	62
What you are about to witness	63
Since 2011, Melbourne, Australia, has	64
For him every month is	65
She lived in the moment and had no sense of history.	66
After the evening meal	67
Usually, at some time	68
Mindfulness	69
Charlie Parker	70
A man walks into a bar	71
Even from the end of the street	72
It might have been	73
Ritual	74

Words aren't working	75
I have put the child	76
Coronavirusdisease – 2019	77
Love in the time of Corona	78
Take	79
Acknowledgements	80

He hinted he might consider moving

if she promised an ocean, or, at least, a river view. After not hearing from her, he returned to the story and noted the unhandy cadence of its first sentence. He made a promise to himself to rewrite the opening.

When she read the draft of his story, she sent him a river in an envelope. A week later, he received a parcel. When he opened it, an ocean flooded his lounge room. After that, he never heard from her again, and he never did get around to rewriting the beginning, or, for that matter, finishing the

Every river

Every poet has a river
in them, every river
a poem; each ocean
a story; creek
a tale; narrative
running

One wonders

why they reside here
when the deckchairs on
the balconies remain empty
while the river below the
hills storied with houses
is begging to be beheld.

The river – rightly indifferent –
does what rivers do: slips
out unnoticed to the ocean,
birdsong at its back.

They come down

They come down at night
To fish in a river
In which she is yet
To see a fish

She puts on Amy Winehouse
And between tracks
Finds herself longing for
All those songs
Waiting to be sung

no water   no bridge

no bridge   no water
was is   now was
no water   now bridge
now is   no was
now water   no bridge
was was   no is
no water   no bridge

It is yet to be determined

if either of them was familiar with *Adventures of Huckleberry Finn* or other tales of trips down the Mississippi River. (And at this point I would like to add some context to the content of this story by saying that in 1895 Mark Twain made a whistle-stop visit to colonial Australia during a world tour of 150 lectures). After rain, the Merri Creek flowed as quickly as any river, and the two young boys steered the upturned rusty roof of the car down the rapids just as deftly as any Huck or Tom.

There may be some flaws in this story

as Neil couldn't remember how he and Billy got there. They may have hitchhiked as they were too young to drive, and using public transport was not a cool option. And it must have been on a weekend or during the summer school holidays that they ended up in Torquay, a beach resort, on the west coast.

After hours of surfing and sunbaking, they bought some takeaway and went back to where they had set up camp in a copse of tea tree beyond the foreshore. Easing into their sleeping bags, the boys talked about their adventure in a low whisper while the light seeped from the treed retreat.

They woke to a rustling and bustle of possibilities, faint filtering of moonlight. Neil's active imagination let in flashing scenes of slasher movies. Billy thought of nocturnal animals. If a dog were nearby, it would have, at this point, howled. The two girls were giggling as they stumbled through the underbrush. Not long after, the boys' fears of Freddy Krueger and foxes were sweetly assuaged when the girls slipped into their sleeping bags.

Right now they missed lying

on summer lawns, listening to the night choir of crickets and singing Dylan. So, when the tail lights of the semi-trailer suddenly brightened, and they heard the gradual lowering of gears, it was like a major chord change in a song waiting to be sung.

It was meant to be a time of rebellion. They were 16, maybe 17, and it was, after all, the 60s. Sydney was a long way from Melbourne, so, longitudinally, hitchhiking some 560 miles from one city to another would be a far-out act of apostasy. After dark, they thumbed down a semi on Sydney Road, and instantly their adventure had begun. It ended about 60 miles up the Hume Highway when the driver needed to detour to Shepparton. They wanted to be on the road and hip like Jack Kerouac, but there was no semblance of cool sitting in a bus shelter in Seymour waiting for a lift to take them to the glittering city in the north. After several failed attempts to hitch a ride, they decided to cross the highway.

The semi took a few hundred yards to stop, but they were already running towards it. They climbed into the cabin and thanked the truckie for the lift. He was a man of few words and remained laconic when he was pulled over by the police just outside of Kilmore. 'Hide these,' he said, throwing them two small plastic bottles.

They left the Thumpin' Tum discotheque after the Purple Hearts set. Where once they hitchhiked the seven miles from the city to Preston, they now walked home. Sometimes, after taking pills, they thought of the truck driver. They hoped he was doing okay, wherever he was.

It was in the days before streets

were modified with speed humps to slow traffic. On rainy days the two friends raced icy pole sticks down the flooding gutters. They got used to speeding cars and distinguishing between sounds made by the gearboxes of different vehicles.

As children, they shared everything, and later, in adolescence, even loved the same woman.

When older, one moved to the country, married and owned an automatic Audi A6, while the other remained single, continued to live in suburbia and drove a manual Mazda 2. They never saw each other or that girl again.

Leaving the café

she asks where his car is parked. Over there, he replies. Oh, you've a blue hatchback too, she says. That night someone has a dream that two blue cars meet head-on on an unknown stretch of highway and morph into a new model and a new make.

(for Tess)

Sometimes I don't feel comfortable writing

about something which might end tragically, like the time I complacently likened the shrill laughter of teenagers inside the cabin of the speeding vehicle to hubcaps bouncing down a highway before losing control of the narrative and having the head of the driver shatter the windscreen.

Some six hours after meeting

they were having sex. Some ten years earlier, they shared a loss of innocence.

She found his contact details in the exhibition catalogue. She was curious to know if he still had that painting he did for her when he was in Year 11. He knew the one. It was a clumsy depiction of a supermarket car park in the manner of Jeffrey Smart.

In his reply email, he detailed how he had used the back of the painting – the other side of the Masonite – to paint a portrait of his wife. She would have seen it, he told her. It was one of the works in the exhibition.

He searched his inbox until he found the email from two years ago. He contacted her and asked if she was still interested in that painting he did for her all those years ago. No, he said, his marriage had not endured. Yes, she said, she was seeing someone, but it was early doors. And, yes, she typed, she knew where the car park was. It had not changed in a decade.

It's not that he still didn't desire

women. He did. He couldn't help but. But, of late, seduction had become so perfunctory that he solicited his psyche to identify scenarios to quicken his cupidity.

He had recently graduated with majors in history and geography but had no interest in applying his knowledge of those subjects in either the academic or mercantile worlds. Instead, he moved on the idea his mind had unearthed to climax his conquests.

Through his studies, he knew there were nearly 200 countries in the world. What if – as his mind suggested – he was to set himself the task of seducing a woman from each and every country?

Very quickly, he was imagining himself as a gondolier taxiing the canals of Venice; a Norwegian navigating the Northwest Passage; an 18th-century libertine queueing to enter the Catacombes de Paris.

It had to start somewhere, according to Jarvis Cocker, so he started it there at the supermarket when he artfully nudged his shopping trolley into hers. He was pleased to hear she wasn't Greek (not that it matters) or that she studied sculpture (not that that mattered either). He was more pleased to know that she was from Melbourne and – less so – studying for a Bachelor of Marine Science. The most important thing to him was to start his crusade locally.

The journey to the bedroom from – in this case – the checkout aisle was, as always, a seamless... I was about to say exercise, but that would suggest that some sort of effort was required. This is not so with our Lothario. He has never had any trouble getting to this point, but now the no trouble part of seduction was what troubled him the most.

He could not say for certain when he started getting into character. It may have been when her hand feathered his as they manoeuvred their trolleys after meeting in Aisle 8. Or when the middle-aged checkout woman sheepishly smiled – then blushed – at the theatrical way he paywaved for his grocery items. But, by the time the couple left the supermarket, he had convinced himself he was a 19th-century explorer on a trip into the interior of Australia.

The early reports from the car park that his imagination fed back to him were promising. And when, in the dimly lit bedroom, she disrobed, there was nothing in the first sighting to dispel Charles Sturt's theory of, or dissolve our Lothario's belief in, the existence of a large inland sea.

disspooned

he rests the soles
of his feet on
her calves

then walks into
her dreams

Friends asked her

if she had made a New Year's resolution. Yes, she answered, she had. She hoped not to lose any more weight, or to stabilise it, at least. But she knew this was a forlorn hope as she had witnessed her brothers and sisters make the same wish and fail.

Like her siblings, she was genetically predisposed to a condition that curtailed existence. Her brother had resided in a cool climate and outlasted his sisters, who preferred the more tropical zones. She could have Googled to determine if there was any scientific evidence supporting the theory that being in a temperate environment contributed to longevity. However, as the differential between the timespan of her siblings was minimal, she chose to exist in ignorance. And bliss.

He took her in his hand and forced her onto his skin. He was methodical and predictable with his manoeuvres, but she felt both comfortable and satisfied with the inevitability of his movements. She had been over every part of his body except his back. She never did get to explore that region of his anatomy.

He had an open marriage, so she doubted he would ever leave his wife. She blithely accepted the conditions of the relationship and bore no grudges against her. She even enjoyed the occasional throupling, which usually took place after he and his wife returned from a day on the beach, their bodies sweaty, skin speckled with sand.

Although she felt her fate was literally in his hands, she knew that, in fact, it was going to be her who would end the relationship. When the time came, she would be content with the little that was left as she slowly slid down the shower plughole.

When the quiz show host

asks the question, the contestant is unsure if the answer will be an educated guess or a stab in the dark. The contestant takes too long thinking and, barely beating the countdown clock, lets fly with an uncultured swish.

He thought the opening line

of the story was witty and fetching. *They bring nothing to the table – except cards. What people usually bring to a table in a café or restaurant is patronage and the given custom of ordering and paying for food and drink* was the intended next sentence. While tourists feasted on tapas or *jamón*, the *madrileñas* served game after game of canasta. The author finished his meal and sangria, settled the bill and left the café clutching his notepad with the unfinished story.

The clock in the hotel room reads 11.56 as the author closes the notepad on the first draft of his story and turns off the bedside lamp. Four minutes later – on the stroke of midnight – the women in the café order four glasses of cava and *racions* of seafood to share.

It is hoped this story

will appeal to those interested in the four humours of Hippocratic medicine, which was the commonly held view of the human body among European physicians until the advent of modern medical research in the 19th century.

In the first decade of the 20th century, the Irish writer James Joyce – either frustrated with its conventional structure or furious at publishers who ignored it – tossed the manuscript of *Stephen Hero* into a fire. Apparently, his wife, Nora, and his sister, Eileen, saved part of the document which would later be retitled *A Portrait of the Artist as a Young Man*.

In the same decade of the 21st century, a frustrated and furious Australian writer threw the pages of his poetry manuscript into the Southern Ocean.

At the same time, a Latin American writer – either frustrated or furious – was surreptitiously slipping the notebooks containing his short stories into his own coffin which would soon be lowered into a grave in Cartagena de Indias.

Meanwhile, an English writer – neither frustrated nor furious – was systematically saving the versions of everything he wrote to the cloud.

Imagine if you can this story

beginning at 8.16 a.m. on a Friday when the middle-aged vice-president of an insurance company (immaculately attired in a three-piece pinstripe suit) is walking to his office in a city in Connecticut. Try to picture a casually dressed non-mercantile man walking along the same street in the opposite direction the next morning to, perhaps, purchase a newspaper. See how both men drop a piece of paper they have, at that moment, taken out of their trouser pockets. How both bend over to retrieve the paper scraps from the sidewalk, then look at what is in their hands.

One note reads, money is a kind of poetry. The other, poetry is the supreme fiction.

If there were a need for a story

it would be to say that *One Hundred Years of Solitude* was on the list of 100 books to read before you die. While I have no recollection of the Buendía family and what magic happens in the town of Macondo, I will never forget the day of the book signing and the Colombian writer slowly closing my copy of the novel and gently pushing it towards me before leaning over and whispering, 'What matters in life is not what happens to you but what you remember and how you remember it.'

This turns out to be

a noticeably short story as it is being narrated by a woman who is reluctant to continue as she fears she may have told it before.

Rothko

the more we look the more we see
the more we see the more we look

Tanka

from ennui
he turns on the TV –
a silent witness
to the slow killing
in nature's colosseum

The landscape

watched the train pass on its long journey and silently rejoiced as the last carriage and its passengers disappeared from view.

Far off the world

Far off, the world
is burning. Here,
early evening, in
hazy light, birds
trill and chirp.
A gentle summer breeze
bringing fragments
of flowers,
ash.

I really shouldn't

complain. I mean, it's not a bad life. I get to fly frequently and travel over beautiful lakes and some of the greenest countryside in the world. If things go my way, I also get to spend a little time on the sands of exclusive beach resorts and observe the local birdlife. I admit I like to play around occasionally, so I have a personal assistant who keeps me in the best condition. I am often introduced to celebrities who address me in the most courteous manner and treat me with respect even when my behaviour is (as it can sometimes be) errant.

So, no, I shouldn't complain. However, in my defence, I have to say that there are times when I believe I have been driven to conduct unbecoming. Was it my fault that I got lost in the woods at Augusta and nearly drowned at Pebble Beach? Even, above or below, sometimes the behaviour of these oddly dressed guys is so unprofessional and totally below par.

She had positioned herself

in society so as to be able to write full time, and had published several books, including a new and selected. Her poems were usually about love and loss and longing, and she had nurtured a reputation as a major minor poet. She was quite content with her achievement to date but now she had writer's block. She had not written a poem in over a year.

As she lived in a leafy outer suburb, a literary friend suggested she try her hand at ecopoetry. The poems came – as Keats said they should – as naturally as leaves to a tree. Within a matter of months, she had enough for a manuscript. After ringing her agent to discuss her new book, she went outside and commenced cultivating her garden, using the pages of her manuscript as compost.

Maybe we should cut

the lyrical I some slack, but we'll see what happens. After all, the lyrical I (the he of this story) doesn't know much about poetry and literature, and yet the audience at his panel discussion on 'Divorce & the Hereafter' was smitten when he dropped the words allegory, analogy, parable and metaphor into his exhaustive introductory speech to describe his long and tormented voyage. However, the discerning audience member would have picked up on the word liked and silently chided him for not using the word simile when comparing his life to a slowly sinking ship.

If he knew anything about literature, he would have realised that he could have pulled his life into some semblance of order by being less ignorant of the more traditional forms of poetry like the sonnet. (At one stage, I felt like calling out that the haiku might have helped, briefly.) And little did the poor sap know that it was the pantoum that would have saved his marriage. In fact, pantoums are all I write, and my relationship with my wife is as tight as a drum.

His limited knowledge of literary tradition and genres was his undoing. All he knew of poetry was *vers libre* – and that's what sank him.

Simileless

i am lost
for words
and have
nothing
to liken
lichen to

Fall

autumn wind
cyclists in lycra
riding in italics

Speech therapy

tired of talkback
she puts on music
then starts talking

She said,

for someone who writes poetry, you sure don't say much.

He said, the silence between words carries as much weight as the words themselves.

The next day, she cleared out her wardrobe and left a scrap of paper on the kitchen table on which she had written a two-word poem.

At first I thought

the girl on the tram sitting opposite was smiling at something on her phone. A text message from her lover, perhaps. Then I sensed she might be looking in my direction.

'Hey, that's a cool T-shirt,' she said in a soft voice.

My T-shirt is black, featuring a black and white facial image with a shock of white hair and sunglasses. Those not 'in the know' would just see it as a feline creature with some human characteristics. However, I don't wear it for the unsuspecting masses, but rather for those (of which this woman was one) who would 'get' the anthropomorphic image.

'It's funny, you know, because I don't really like Andy Warhol, and I especially don't like cats,' I said.

'Then, why do you wear the T-shirt?'

'Because, as you say, it's cool.'

What followed was an animated discussion about Warhol's aesthetics. I dismissed his facile nihilism and amoral cynicism, while she lauded his take on consumerism and celebrity culture. I said he had no apparent ideological imperative. She said he would be the first to admit it. So we agreed to disagree, both smiling at the consensus. And there was no talk of cats.

At this point, I would like to confess that I'm a bit of a T-shirt tragic. Along with the Warhol tee, my favourites are the Hunter S. Tomcat, Cat Sabbath, and the one of a squirrel wearing an aviator flying cap with goggles. Squirrel Biggles I call him.

The next day I chose to stick with the moggy theme and wear the Hunter S. Tomcat tee. The tram had only travelled a few stops when I got the feeling that I was being observed by a nearby passenger. I knew that if they were going to say something, I had a fair idea what it was – and what my response would be.

Ask you (said quickly)

I can't get it to go
Upright. It lies on its side
And no amount of coaxing
Will make it erect.
Sometimes things aren't black
And white. Sometimes they're grey
And despite the fingering
It refuses to rise.
It's like a game of cat
And mouse, and the mouse
Loses, and the cat (hopefully
Out of the bag by now) is content
To lie there with me with a bucket
Of popcorn and view
The moving world obliquely.

Post Pompeii, Hiroshima, Apocalypse

at that moment
captured in acts
of standing
or walking
or sitting
heads lowered
hands near-clasped
(as if!) in prayer

In the zone

Leaning over, she
asks if I mind having
the blind up, then
resumes her seat.
The sun warms my shoulder.
And for the remainder of
the journey she sits motion-
less with lowered head,
thumbs tapping text
into her phone.

There are several scars in this story

and stories in the scars. She starts with his face.
'This one on your eyebrow. How did you get that?'
'In a fight,' he answers.
'Were you a boxer?'
'No,' he says. 'I got in a fight in secondary school.'
'Did you win?'
'By a TKO,' he answers, gently tapping her temple with his fist.
'And this one?' she asks, fingering the raised line of skin on his chin.
'That was from playing football.'
'Were you any good?'
'I have a couple of trophies somewhere.'

Having first seen her in the bar the previous evening, he would email his manager to say he could feel a cold coming on and wouldn't be in the office the next day.

The exploration of his body continued.

He tells her that the blemish on his upper arm was caused by a knife blade rather than a tetanus shot he had when a child.

She slides her hand down his chest until her finger rests in the small hollow in his abdomen where his appendix was removed.

'I've got one too,' she says, taking his hand and placing it on the corresponding part of her anatomy.

He bends his right leg so she can see the mark on the outside of his knee. Again, he forsakes fact for fiction and replaces a bicycle accident for a bullet in Afghanistan.

'You've led a dangerous life, haven't you, my brave little soldier?'

He will face his toughest battle when his wife finds the sext messages on his smartphone.

He loved live theatre and bled easily.

She had never had a blood nose and preferred the cinema.
He was gifted with a hand that wrote in a cursive script.
Most of her messages were by text.
There was a significant age difference and they frequently argued.

On one occasion, after a heated exchange, he commenced writing a letter seeking her forgiveness for his behaviour the previous evening. By mid-morning the temperature was already 30 degrees Celsius. Before he could lift a finger to depress the left nostril a trickle of blood dropped onto the third page of his letter. He looked down at the blurred script, the broken narrative. With his thumb he smeared blood on all the pages to give his story more gravitas.

After reading the first sentence of his letter, she decided to end the relationship and left the house to see a film. *Nosferatu* was showing at her local cinema. A week later, she started dating a vampire.

'What side of the bed do you want?' he asked her.

'What do you mean?' she replied.
'Left, or right?'
'Depends on which way you're looking at the bed.'
'Head to foot.'
'We haven't even done anything yet.'
'I'm thinking of afterwards.'
'Does it matter?'
'I just have a preference, that's all,' he said, removing his shoes.
'Is it that important?'
'I have a medical condition.'
'A medical condition?'
'I need to lie on my right side on the right-hand side of the bed.'

'That means then that you'll be right next to the bedroom door,' she said, reclasping her bra. 'So, when you put your shoes back on, you go out that door and turn right, and you'll find the front door. And if it's all right with you, would you please lock the door when you've left.'

Back then he was mesmerised by them –

the talented and less talented who appeared on the numerous singing talent shows on TV. Both the judges and the audience seemed particularly fascinated by female voices that could sustain vowel sounds for an inordinate length of time. Some acts were given standing ovations while others met with drop-jawed looks of disbelief from the judges. He had trouble distinguishing between what was considered good and what was deemed not so good. But what he did know was that love only has one syllable.

After watching several hours of recorded shows, he fell asleep in his chair. Later, he would say that he couldn't recall if he was woken by a dream or the sound of a prolonged wailing note.

The following day, he returned from work to find the apartment complex cordoned off. The death of the promising young singer next door was being treated as suspicious.

The pimple was pissed off

that it erupted on the neck, as it would have much preferred to have surreptitiously and softly surfaced on an unexposed slither of skin. Yet here it was, beyond its control, obvious and angry. The pimple looked out from its epidermal knoll. The rest is history.

White angels

In twilight moments
He numbers them,

Like counting sheep.
But he's not enticing sleep

(Although he nods off anywhere:
A couch; a car; a chair.)

And today as we take tea
He says he's counted seventy-three.

Seventy-three different
White cabbage butterflies,

Or the same butterfly
Seventy-three times?

No matter, to him, they're
His very own white angels

Which hover over his roses
In the early summer sun.

To sleep, perchance

My father falls asleep at the drop
Of a hat, or where he imagines
        A hat to be.
The nurse tells my sister to 'be prepared'.
My sister tells me that she never dreams,
        But that night,
In her sleep, our father is walking
Towards her wearing sunglasses.
        My sister wakes.

My father is still sleeping.

Requiem

Our daily walk takes longer now.
But you still insist on
Passing through the cemetery
With its ever-growing
Number of headstones.
You taught her grandmother
When we lived in Warrnambool
You tell me again. And his son,
You repeat, never returned from
The war in Vietnam.
And, as is our habit, we stop
To rest at the rotunda
Where, as usual, you turn
Away from the babies' graves.
And I respectfully deflect
The trembling requiem.

We ask

We ask to
We ask to be
We ask to be able to
We ask that we be able to
To move on
To move on with our lives
That we be able to move on
To move on and to find closure
To. Find. Closure.

She took a seat

in the waiting room, hoping to be seen soon. Tempting as it was to pick up one of the magazines and read about the split of Brangelina and the peccadilloes of other celebs, she chose instead to look out the window. Amongst the crowd on the pavement was a young man who appeared to be moving in slow motion compared to other pedestrians. He kept looking over his shoulder, but no one seemed to notice him or, for that matter, the falling woman and the figure flying above their heads.

She heard a name being called and turned her gaze to the waiting room only to see a naked man rising from his chair.

The sleeper woke before she would be given a chance to leave the room and enter the dream.

Always

There is regret. Always there is regret – Philip Larkin

Love has its wires and
sorrow fences. But,
regret's a colt running
free with brumbies,
eschewing pasture,
cantering into
desuetude of
its own flesh.

The sea (is dead)

The sea is dead to me, you said,
If there were no waves.
If there were no swell,
Well, the ocean was dead. To me
You were the Dead Sea
I got to see inside of me.
I remained, and remain, calm
So your (dis)appearance was a mystery.
There was no surfing or swimming,
And, certainly, no waves or waving.
So, if there were no waves,
Why was the sea not dead to you?
The dead see the Dead Sea.

From the moment

he entered the world, he had been pushed around. At least, that's how it felt. From infancy until now – the twilight years – he had had no control over where he went or what he did.

He understood the inherent powerlessness of confinement to the cradle, and the inevitable impotency leading to the grave, but what of the years between? What had he done for himself in all that time?

Time? It was running out. Sure, he had worked on a PhD in his youth, marked student exam papers in his middle years, and later contributed to government policy. All this might have been important to other people, but it gave him no pleasure or satisfaction. Nowadays, against what little will he had, he found himself compiling shopping lists and tackling word puzzles in the daily newspapers.

Then, when all seemed lost, his luck seemed to change. He was finally doing something he enjoyed, something which interested him. All was going well until the fourth paragraph when he began to feel the life force leav

Being smaller than the other two

he knew it would only be a matter of time before they ganged up on him. What he didn't anticipate was that his big brother would team with M.W. to bully and torment him.

He was powerless to stop the abuse which felt like it had been going on for an eternity. It was as if the very air in his lungs was being sucked out. He was on the brink of exhaustion and total collapse.

The only thing that gave Small Magellanic Cloud comfort was the fact that it would take Large Magellanic Cloud and Milky Way several billion years to wipe him off the face of the universe.

What you are about to witness

may vary marginally from other street sightings.

She has her hand to her ear, head bowed. She is not talking, but her lips move slightly as she listens intently to the voice on the other end. Her face is giving nothing away; the identity of the unheard caller endless with possibilities for inquisitive passers-by.

As he leans over, he sees that it is, in fact, a small transistor radio pressed to the side of her head, and he instantly recognises the voice of the ABC morning presenter as he drops several gold coins into the cup.

Since 2011, Melbourne, Australia, has

often been named the world's most liveable city. Its central business district is renowned for its laneways and its alfresco dining. It also has several lanes, such as AC/DC and Hosier, which feature street art. Here, you won't find work known as tagging, but art by acclaimed street artists such as Banksy. A number of Banksy stencils have been damaged or destroyed by deliberate and inadvertent acts. Some argue that these artefacts are great cultural losses, others that street art is not owned by anyone and is, by nature, ephemeral. However, a discussion such as this belongs in another story.

In this story, I want to tell you of the time I visited Melbourne in 2016 and, while on a tour of its laneways, came across a one-line story by American writer Alex Epstein scribbled on a wall. The story is called 'Fiction' and it goes, 'And the last man in the world is writing a novel.' Underneath the story, written in a different hand, is 'So, obviously, he will have to self-publish.' And underneath that, in yet another script, is the quote, 'What's the intended print run?'

The last story in *Lunar Savings Time* – the same book in which 'Fiction' appears – is called 'Compendium of Most Snowflakes', and it too is comprised of one line which reads, 'The last man in the world wrote the last haiku in the world.' I thought that was especially clever, as everybody knows poetry doesn't sell.

For him every month is

you know like cruel like it is now in april with the sun beating down on his face in jack kerouac alley & later when theres like you know no sun theres city lights & its like wow look at the lights man & then its like another alley another lane another whatever (but that's like what he likes coz its not cool @ home you know) & then from the second level of vesuvio i see his t-shirt I EAT PUSSY LIKE A KID EATS CAKE & i think thats like not cool man & how mallarmé you know wanted like removed from the lexicon & as i point my iphone @ you a voice behind me says hey you know that aint cool dude & hes you know more than like right you know

She lived in the moment and had no sense of history.

She also once had an eye for property and a liking for spices. She owned houses and apartments in many countries – including her birthplace, Holland – but lost them all when the global financial crisis hit. She now lived in a tenement in Manhattan. She once owned the tenement but had offloaded it to an Englishman for a small Indonesian island to mitigate her debt. It was a condition of the property exchange that the Dutchwoman live with the Englishman.

She was in the kitchen adding nutmeg and other spices to the evening meal. When she heard the door open she knew what was coming. 'Hi, hon, I'm home.' First, the sound of the fridge door opening and closing, the top coming off a bottle of beer, then footsteps on the tiled floor. Standing over the cooktop, she felt her body brace itself for when he would place his hand on her hip, lean over her shoulder, sniff and whisper, 'Trying to spice up our lives, eh?'

Then, over time, she lost the taste for spices. She would spend the rest of her life on Pulau Run.

After the evening meal

he sidles to the comfort of his lounge room chair with his glass of wine and studies her standing over the kitchen sink. It seems it is slowly rather than suddenly that the sun strikes the window and streams through it.

At other times, he will observe her sewing, looking at a map, or nonchalantly (or not) looking over her left shoulder, a pearl earring glinting.

It will take him a lifetime to know that while she can at times be possessed, he will never possess her.

Usually, at some time

the next day, she recounts the latter part of the film they watched the previous night because, usually, for most of the time, he is drunk.

One morning, she makes up a happy ending, and, as usual, he believes her.

Mindfulness

And unlike Tarzan I'm not buff
or you a comely Hollywood Jane

And I'm trying not to swing from
vine to vine (or if I do
taking it one vine at a time)
but learning how to find the
clearing by simply being here

And I haven't learnt my lines
for the next scene or
if you are and/or I am in it…

And I see no ending

Charlie Parker

one time
he hocked
his horn
to hire
a horse
to woo
his girl
and win
her back

A man walks into a bar

and takes up a stool next to someone holding a glass of red wine.

'What can I get you?' the bartender asks the man who has just sat down.

'I think I'll have what he's having,' the man says, gesturing in the direction of the figure next to him, who looks like a Renaissance depiction of Yahweh.

The bartender serves the man a glass of water.

Even from the end of the street

in the fading light of dusk, he immediately recognised them. Not the individuals as such, but the group. He had seen a similar one before, and he knew their look and modus operandi. They would gather in the street, then split into pairs and head in different directions, their hands concealing arsenal under jackets and coats.

He parked the car down from his house just as the mob was dispersing. Then he rang his wife and told her to lock the front door and close the curtains, and that he would use the nearby alley to enter the house from the rear. He also told her to turn off her mobile phone and computer.

They stood a few paces from the front door, tightly holding onto each other. Neither of them was religious, but they both found themselves saying silent prayers when the doorbell rang. They waited, but there were no more chimes. Then they heard footsteps retreating down the path and to the pavement.

When they next turned on their computers, they waited for their eyes to be inevitably drawn to the flashing ads on the right-hand side of the screen. Sure enough, they were there, but instead of seeing reminders of their latest Google searches, here were images of *Awake!* and *Watchtower*.

It might have been

the sound of lawnmowers, as his neighbours cut their lawns with the accustomed regularity of the migratory flights of birds.

The skies were burdened with dark clouds, but the wind and the rain of the past few days, which had menaced and hampered man and machine, were now moving out to the Indian Ocean.

The moment was now.

But, at that moment, no men with mowers manifested on lawns. No machinery shrieked from unsighted sheds. Instead, sparrows twitched and skipped into hedges, magpies swooped through tree branches.

From his armchair, he thought he could see a pelican on high riding a thermal current. But he had not seen the majestic birds this far down the river since his wife died.

Then the noise ceased, and the pelican went beyond the clouds.

Ritual

Good Friday
        Lawnmowers
Easter Monday
        Leaf blowers

Words aren't working

After Tomas Tranströmer's *From March '79*

Words aren't working when a line
From Tranströmer finds a way into my poem.
Not that I'm all that sure it belongs
Here as it's very European.
But it leaves its mark in the text anyway
Like the tracks of reindeer in snow.
Then the snow melts to reveal
A desert and the paw
Prints of a kangaroo
For as far as the eye can see,
Far as the ear can hear.

I have put the child

to sleep, she said, getting into bed.

Just like James Joyce boasted what he did with language, he said, turning off the light.

The parents woke early the next morning to discover a note pinned to the head of the cot and the child missing.

Coronavirusdisease – 2019

On my walk it stalks me.
Playful as a pup, it flits
and skips in the clippings
from yesterday's mowing of
the reserve behind my house.
Dancing in front or back,
it maintains its social distancing,
the wagtail's tail wagging like
a scripting quill. The sound of its call
like muted keys of a typewriter,
touch typing on a keyboard.

I miss the feel of you
and the sound of your voice.

Love in the time of Corona

There are
so many books
that I would like
to touch
and open…

And then
there are people,
too.

Take

At times hunted
with both hands
captured and

carried to
a godless or
safe place

Or ingested
for pleasure
or pain

Or determined

Whatever
it is care
and we should
take it

Acknowledgements

Poems and flash fiction pieces from this collection have appeared in the following publications, some of them as earlier versions.

101 Words (USA), *Australian Poetry Members Anthology 2014*, *Bluepepper*, *Coolabah* (Spain), *Cordite*, *The Husk* (USA), *Inscribe*, *Musing During a Time of Pandemic Anthology* (Kenya), *Oxygen*, *Permafrost* (USA), *RumbleFish* (USA), *Short and Twisted*, *Southerly*, *Star 82 Review* (USA), *The Victorian Writer*.

All photos by Ray Liversidge and Terri Redpath.

www.ingramcontent.com/pod-product-compliance
Lightning Source LLC
Chambersburg PA
CBHW071429130526
44590CB00064B/2833